SIMPLY SUSHI

HINKLER
BOOKS

Creative Director: Sam Grimmer

Editor: Jasmine Chan

Design: Katherine Power

Photography: Ned Meldrum

First published in 2004
by Hinkler Books Pty Ltd
17-23 Redwood Drive
Dingley Victoria 3172 Australia
www.hinklerbooks.com

Printed and bound in China
Reprinted 2005

HINKLER
BOOKS

ISBN 1 7412 1972 8

CONTENTS

INTRODUCTION

Irasshai, irasshaimase ...Welcome! This spirited and warm greeting is what you first hear when arriving at the sushi shop and is indeed the itamae-san, the sushi chef, welcoming you.

Itamae means 'in front of the chopping board' and implies that the chef is indeed that person who is always at the board ready for action!

There are more sushi bars in Japan than any other type of restaurant and the proliferation of Japanese sushi bars in cities all over the world has led to an enormous interest in this delightfully appetising food.

The basic elements of Japanese cuisine are always constant: a Japanese meal is traditionally restrained in quantity, excellent in quality and elegant in presentation.

The Japanese style of eating is dependent on the freshest ingredients in season and emphasises natural flavours and minimal animal fats. The emphasis on fresh food is part of the deep respect for nature that is so important in Japanese culture. It is believed that the products of the earth and sea should be prepared in ways that preserve their natural forms and flavours as much as possible so as to show off their own special character. Often food is simply presented but always a delight to the eyes as well as the taste buds.

Sushi, more than any other dish, is the consummate example, as it is a presentation of food that is natural, harmonious and aesthetically pleasing. With the Japanese sense for artistic presentation, never before has so little been made to look like so much.

A famous Japanese chef, Tsuji, said: '... food should be prepared so as to do honour to the essence of the ingredients chosen.'

Simply put, sushi combines seasoned rice and a wide variety of seafood and vegetables.

Making sushi is so complicated that it takes years for the professional chef to master—but don't let this put you off. It is also easy enough to be done at home and a complete beginner can master simple sushi making with great success. It doesn't matter if first attempts aren't perfect, making sushi is fun, and even less artistic efforts will taste delicious.

We know sushi is delicious, colourful and an art form. We also know it is very nutritious and comes in many forms. But what are its origins, who invented it, how to eat it and how to make it are common questions and Simply Sushi aims at answering these and more, and offers a comprehensive guide to the art of creating sushi at home.

ORIGINS

hilst sushi is commonly seen as one of the representative foods of Japan, its origins are to be found elsewhere.

History indicates that the origins of sushi practice are in South-East Asia. It then moved to China in the 2nd century AD before being introduced into Japan in the 7th century AD.

In Japan, sushi originated as a way of preserving fish. Long ago, fish was preserved by packing it with cooked rice. During the fermentation process, the rice produced lactic acid, which effectively pickled the fish.

One of the original forms was nare-zushi or funa-zushi, a sushi made with carp in the vicinity of Lake Biwa in Shiga Prefecture. The fish was salted and allowed to mature on a bed of rice, after which the rice was discarded. This preparation was inordinately long and took from two months to more than one year!

In the 15th century, a technique of weighting the sushi with a stone was used to accelerate the fermentation time. This eventually led to the practice of eating both fish and rice. Later development included the addition of vinegar to imitate the tartness of fermented rice.

NOTE:
With no difference in meaning, sushi becomes -zushi, when used in conjunction with certain words

From this point, sushi started to evolve into what we know it to be today. As Japan is an island nation surrounded by seas rich in an assortment of seafood, it has always fed its inhabitants from the sea and the rice fields. Sushi, the combination of raw fish and seasoned rice is a sensible choice of food in Japan. From north to south, countless varieties of sushi developed according to geography and history.

The varieties of sushi known today are based on the one constant ingredient that defines sushi: the rice seasoned with vinegar, sugar and salt, known as sushi-meshi, regardless of whether it is hand-squeezed, rolled in seaweed or pressed into a mould.

THE MAIN TYPES OF SUSHI

NIGIRI-ZUSHI (SQUEEZED)

It is probably fair to say that sushi is best represented in the world by a hand formed style known as nigiri-zushi, or squeezed sushi. Typically these are small fingers of rice with a topping of mostly raw seafood, served in pairs at the sushi bar. It is also known as Edomae-zushi as it was first made in Edo, as Tokyo was known prior to 1868.

MAKI-ZUSHI (ROLLED)

For maki-zushi, a sheet of toasted nori seaweed is spread with a layer of seasoned rice and strips of seafood and/or vegetables etc are arranged on top. The whole is then rolled and cut into rounds.

CHIRASHI-ZUSHI (SCATTERED)

Chirashi-zushi is seafood and vegetables in or on vinegared rice, typically served in lacquered bowls. It is certainly the easiest type of sushi to make and indeed is made in all kitchens in Japanese homes.

OSHI-ZUSHI (PRESSED)

Literally translated, oshi-zushi means press moulded sushi. Typically, the desired garnishes, often cooked or marinated seafood, are placed on the bottom of the mould. This is topped with the sushi rice and then pressed down to firm. The pressed sushi is then removed from the mould, turned upright and cut into bite size pieces.

MAZE-ZUSHI (MIXED)

Some sushi that is regarded as picnic, festival, lunch or snack food that doesn't fit into the above, falls into this category. Two examples are inari-zushi and fukusa-zushi. Inari-zushi consists of deep fried bean curd pouches stuffed with sushi-meshi. For fukusa-zushi, a square of paper-thin omelette is used for wrapping the rice.

Basic Essentials For The Sushi Kitchen

Equipment

These are the most important utensils needed for the preparation of sushi and are readily available from specialist Japanese stores or Asian food markets. Certain tools are not always necessary but make the work a lot easier. Often, suitable alternatives may be found in every kitchen.

Hangiri (wooden bowl)

This is a shallow, broad based wooden tub made of Japanese cypress used for preparing the seasoned rice. Being porous, it absorbs any excess moisture and is perfect for cooling the rice and ensuring the right degree of stickiness and gloss. Substitute with any glass, china or wooden bowl but avoid metal. Choose the largest bowl available to aid in the proper working of the rice and to allow the rice to be spread in a thin layer to cool.

Shamoji (spatula)

These are flat, wooden and round ended spoons used to turn and spread the sushi rice whilst cooling it. Substitute with any broad, flat spoon.

Uchiwa (fan)

This a flat hand-held fan used to cool the rice by encouraging evaporation. Cooling the rice is important to ensure correct texture and gloss. Substitute with cardboard or folded newspaper.

Makisu (bamboo mat)

This is a mat made from thin bamboo sticks woven together with cotton and is essential for the preparation of many forms of rolled sushi. After use, sushi mats must be washed carefully to remove any foodstuffs between the sticks and dried well prior to storage.

MANAITA (CHOPPING BOARD)

Essential for performing a variety of tasks. Traditionally made of wood, but nowadays many people prefer chopping boards made of plastic or resin and whilst not aesthetically pleasing, they are easier to keep clean and free of odour. Choose a large, stable board and always secure by using a damp cloth or rubber non slip matting underneath.

KNIVES

Always try to purchase the best knives you can afford.

Professional sushi chefs use knives which are produced as an outgrowth of forging swords from a single piece of carbon steel. The blades are hard and extremely sharp and are perfect for cutting clean and precise slices. Stainless steel knives are the popular choice for domestic kitchens and are generally adequate for slicing fish for sushi and sashimi. A European meat slicer can do the same basic jobs. Do not use a serrated knife or electric knife as these can tear the flesh and destroy the appearance. Choose one which is long and slender and very sharp. Care for your knives by keeping them in a knife block or special rack. Remember, a dull knife requires much more time and effort than a sharp blade and will always yield a poor result.

RICE COOKER

Whilst the basic utensils have changed little and most cooks still prefer to use traditional utensils, it is worthwhile to invest in an electric rice cooker as it makes perfect rice every time. They are readily available and come in various sizes. Substitute with an appropriate sized pot with a tight fitting lid.

TWEEZERS

These are used to remove small bones from fish. Large, straight-ended tweezers are preferable and readily available at most kitchenware retail outlets. Ask for 'fish' tweezers.

IMPORTANT INGREDIENTS

There is no limitation to the ingredients you may choose to use when making sushi and within the vast range available, there are some that need special mention, as they play an important role in the successful outcome of your sushi. Remember to always choose the very freshest food for making sushi.

SU (RICE VINEGAR)

Japanese rice vinegar is the only one to use for making your sushi, as it is mild tasting and sweet. Western and Chinese vinegars are much more acidic and are too strong and will overpower the delicate flavours of your sushi. Mitsukan brand vinegar is most suitable and readily available from Asian groceries and good supermarkets.

SHOYU (SOY SAUCE)

Japanese soy sauce is an essential ingredient to Japanese food. Made from soy beans, wheat and salt, it is naturally fermented and results in a dark and salty sauce which is one of the primary seasonings in Asian cooking. There are two basic types: usukuchi (light) and koikuchi (dark). Usukuchi is clearer and thinner than koikuchi, but it is also saltier. The darker koikuchi is the one used as a dipping sauce for sushi and sashimi and is readily purchased at supermarkets. Kikkoman and Yamasa brand of soy sauce are recommended. Do not use Chinese soy sauce as it is saltier and more viscous than shoyu. Once opened, soy sauce should be stored in a cool place or refrigerated.

WASABI (JAPANESE HORSERADISH)

Often referred to as Japanese horseradish, this biting yet refreshing spice is a different plant to Western horseradish, being more fragrant and less sharp. There are two kinds of wasabi: sawa wasabi and seiyo wasabi. The botanical name of sawa wasabi is wasabia japonica, an original plant of Japan, also known as mountain hollyhock. This is the fresh wasabi root that is so very difficult to obtain. The English name of seiyo wasabi is horseradish, an original plant of Northern Europe. It is readily available as a powder, available in small round tins and must be mixed with a little cold water to form a paste. Let stand for ten minutes before using to allow flavour to develop. Seiyo wasabi is also available as a ready made paste in a tube, but whilst convenient, its colour and flavour isn't regarded as well.

GARI (PICKLED GINGER)

Sushi is always accompanied by thin slices of pickled ginger—its sharp flavour is perfect to cleanse the palate between mouthfuls of different types of sushi.

It is commonly available pre-prepared in packets or jars in Japanese food stores or Asian markets.

NORI (SEAWEED)

This particular seaweed was first cultivated in Tokyo bay in the seventeenth century and after harvesting is washed, dried, toasted and packaged as wafer thin sheets ready for making sushi rolls. They come in a standard size, 22.5 x 17.5 cm. The sheets are dark green to black in colour, the darker nori being more expensive but with more flavour. It is known as laver Porphyra spp. Toasting the nori sheets over a low heat improves the flavour and texture. Once opened, it should be stored in a sealed container or is best kept in the freezer. Nori is commonly available in supermarkets already pre-toasted and known as Yaki-nori.

SHIITAKE (MUSHROOM)

These mushrooms are available fresh or dried. The fresh mushroom is used for its appearance and soft texture, whereas the dried form offers a more intense flavour and dense quality. When preparing dried shiitake, the mushroom is soaked in tepid water for two hours first and then simmered in a seasoned liquid. The stalks are discarded and the cap is then sliced ready for use.

Dried shiitake keep almost indefinitely in an airtight container and are available in supermarkets.

KAMPYO (SHAVINGS OF DRIED GOURD)

This is an essential ingredient for rolled sushi and much loved by the Japanese. The inner pith of a bottle calabash is shaved into ribbons which are then dried. For sushi, the kampyo is first softened and then cooked in a seasoned liquid. It is commonly available in this finished form at Japanese food stores.

KOMBU (DRIED KELP)

Also a type of seaweed, kombu is sold dried as hard, black sheets and commonly used for the making of dashi or stock, and for flavouring sushi rice.

DASHI (STOCK)

This is a fish stock that underpins so many Japanese dishes and is based on kombu and dried shavings from the fillet of a bonito fish. Nowadays instant dashi granules sold under the name of hon-dashi are commonly used. Simply add 1 teaspoon to 1 litre of simmering water and the resultant stock is ready to use.

KATSUO-BUSHI (DRIED FILLET OF BONITO FISH)

Essential ingredient in the production of dashi, basic soup stock. Packaged dried bonito flakes are called hana-katsuo, flower bonito. They resemble wood shavings and being so thin, release their flavour almost immediately.

MIRIN (SWEET RICE WINE)

This is a heavily sweetened, alcoholic wine made from rice and only used in cooking. It adds a mild sweetness to dishes and as such can be substituted with sugar.

SAKE (JAPANESE RICE WINE)

This is Japan's national beverage and is made by a fermentation process with rice. Not only a traditional drink, Sake is also used as an important ingredient in cooking. Sake comes sweet or dry and can be served cold or warm.

SHISO (PERILLA LEAF)

This attractive herb of the Perilla frutescens plant is related to the mint family and comes available as either a green or red variety. The green leaf is preferred for garnish and used for sushi as it is more fragrant than the red variety. Commonly the seed pods and sprouts are seen to be used as garnish for sashimi. Make sure they are fresh and not wilted.

MAYONNAISE

Japanese mayonnaise is used in some sushi preparations and is a little sweeter and milder than most western brands.

AO-NORI (SEAWEED)

A type of nori different from that used to make sheets. It is known as Enteromorpha spp. It is green in colour and comes as small flakes to sprinkle on food.

TAKUAN (PICKLED RADISH)

A bright yellow, crunchy pickle made from daikon, long white radish. It is commonly thought to aid digestion, especially of fatty foods.

OBORO (FISH FLAKES)

Pink flakes, or powder made from sweetened and cooked white fish. Readily purchased pre-made at Japanese food stores and commonly used in chirashi-zushi.

SASHIMI

When the fish is served on its own, either raw or lightly cooked, it is called sashimi.
To say it is raw is of course correct, but belies the skill and artistry involved in its preparation. The sushi chef is an artist who takes pride in his cutting skills and presentation.

Generally speaking, you can get away with only a few ingredients when making sushi but they need to be absolutely fresh and of the best quality, a fundamental concept to sushi and sashimi. This is particularly true if you use raw seafood for a topping or filling.

The first step then is to purchase your seafood.
If possible, go to the fish markets and tell the fishmonger you need 'sashimi quality' to ensure the best product.

Most fish can be eaten raw but it's best to familiarise yourself with the various types of fish used in sashimi and ask for what is in season. At that time there will be an abundance available, it will also be at its cheapest and most importantly its texture and flavour will be at its best.

Perhaps start only with one or two varieties of fish to practise using.

SELECTING FISH

At the sushi bar, the chef will always purchase seafood whole and then prepare it as required. That way they can ensure that it is in fact the fish they want and can control how to best look after it.

If purchasing whole fish, remember the following points:

1. Fresh fish has a firm flesh that springs back to the touch.
2. Absolutely fresh fish does not have a fishy smell—it should have a pleasant smell of the ocean.
3. The gills should be bright red and moist.
4. Look at the eyes and skin—the eyes should be plump, bright and clear, while the skin should have plentiful scales firmly attached, and be shiny.
5. If required, ask the fishmonger to fillet the fish for you.

If purchasing fillets of fish, remember the following points:

1. Fillets should glisten with moisture and have a good colour appropriate to the type.
2. There should be no brown edges, dried out and curling.
3. The flesh should not be sticky.

Pay attention to the overall quality of the fish shop and the whole fish you see. Start talking with the fishmonger to show your interest. Whichever you choose, be gentle with your fish to avoid bruising or damaging the flesh and always refrigerate it until required. Frozen fish must not be used, as the taste and texture is quite inferior and contradicts the spirit of Japanese cuisine.

SLICING TECHNIQUES

You have been to the market and chosen your fish and now its time to cut it. There are five basic cutting techniques for preparing fish for sashimi and sushi.

Needless to say, a very sharp knife is essential to do the job well. Never 'saw' through the fish. A sushi chef uses a one stroke motion for each slice, pulling the knife towards him.

Any fish can be cut in these forms and served as sashimi. Of particular note is the technique: sogi giri, an angled cut used to yield slices for sushi-dane, or topping, for nigiri-zushi.

With all the following cuts, it is assumed that if the fish was purchased whole, that it has been cut into fillets and then the fillets have had the skin removed, ready for slicing.

Whichever fish you have chosen, there is a basic rule to follow when determining the thickness of cut.

The softer the fish, the thicker the slice; the firmer the fish, the thinner the slice.

You may have to experiment by practicing with a few slices of different thickness. Take a bite out of each and let your mouth help you to decide which is the most appropriate for each type of fish.

HIRA ZUKURI (RECTANGULAR CUT)

This cut is the most useful and applies to all fish. Place fillet across the board in front of you, the thin side closest to you and the thick side furthest away.

Typically you start your slicing on the right hand side of the fish, straight down at a thickness of 1/2–1 cm depending on the fish.

Start at the heel of the knife and finish the cut at the tip of the knife, with a sweeping, drawing motion.

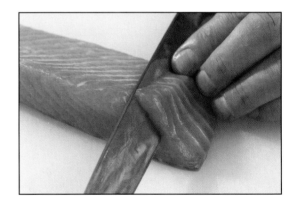

SOGI GIRI (ANGLE CUT)

This is the ideal cut for slices used on nigiri-zushi. If possible start with a rectangular shaped fillet, approximately 7 cm across and 2.5 cm high.

Place fillet across the board in front of you. This time you start slicing from the left hand side.

Measure in from the left side 3 cm and cut down from here at a 45-degree angle, so that the knife meets the bottom left hand edge of the fillet. This will yield a triangular piece of fillet (good for maki-zushi, rolled sushi) and a slanting edge on the left of the fillet.

Continue to slice across the fillet, parallel to and at the same angle as the slanting edge, at a thickness of approximately 1/2–1 cm, depending on the fish.

Usu zukuri (paper thin cut)

This method is mostly suited to firm, white fish such as John Dory or Flounder. Same as the above angle cut except the slices are paper thin, approximately 2 mm in thickness.

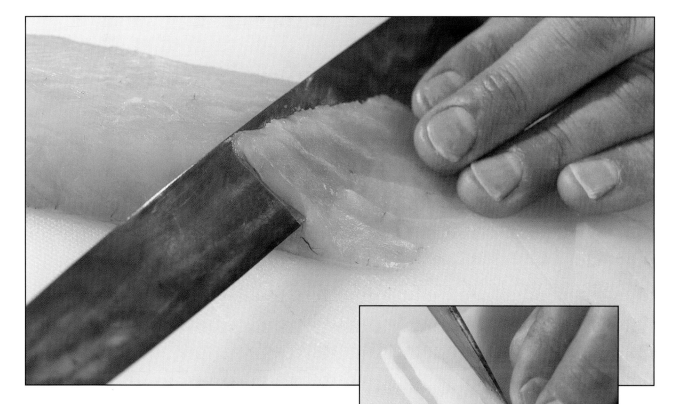

Kaku giri (cube cut)

This cut best suits soft, thick fleshed fish such as tuna, bonito and swordfish.
Cut fillet into strips approximately 2 cm x 2 cm and then cut across the strips every 2 cm to yield dice.

Ito zukuri (thread cut)

This cut is best for squid or white fish with thin fillets like garfish or sand whiting.

Using the tip of the blade, slice across the squid or fish fillets to produce thin strips approximately 1/4 cm wide and 6 cm long.

PRESENTING YOUR SASHIMI

In keeping with the Japanese aesthetic around food, sashimi is most often presented simply with a bowl of shoyu and a small amount of wasabi as the perfect accompaniment.

Commonly the slices are arranged in a row and rested on a bed of finely shredded daikon, or white radish, garnished with a decorative leaf and/or a vegetable curl. A small mound of wasabi is to be found on the right hand side of the plate. Your chosen amount of wasabi is stirred into the shoyu and then the seafood is passed through this before eating.

Sometimes you might choose to present your sashimi slices as a rosette, by overlapping the slices and rolling them up, or putting a few slices together and simply folding them over.

Thread cut of fish can be presented as a small stack and paper thin slices can be arranged directly on the serving plate fanned out.

The garnishes used for sashimi are collectively known as tsuma. They are chosen for their colour, texture and flavour and are meant to be eaten. Carrot and cucumber are common, as are herb leaves, red radish, shredded seaweed and spring onion. Sometimes a simple slice of lemon is seen, or a small mound of grated ginger.

Remember they are a garnish only and shouldn't dominate the plate. One or two is plenty.

Many restaurants also serve their own prepared dipping sauce, a special blend with shoyu as the base ingredient. Two such sauces are Tosa and Ponzu.

Tosa soy sauce

300 ml	soy sauce
100 ml	sake
50 ml	mirin
3 cm	kombu
300 ml	bonito flakes

Combine mirin and sake and burn off the alcohol. Combine all ingredients together and let stand 24 hours. Strain and store in refrigerator. Allow to age to develop flavour.

This basic sauce can also be enhanced with a little freshly squeezed ginger juice or some freshly ground toasted sesame seeds, if that is your preference.

Ponzu sauce

125 ml	lemon juice
60 ml	Japanese rice vinegar
125 ml	soy sauce
20 ml	tamari
30 ml	mirin
5 gm	dried bonito flakes
3 cm square	kombu seaweed

Combine and mix all ingredients well and let stand refrigerated for 24 hours. Strain through muslin cloth. (Fully matures in three months).

SUSHI RICE
(SUSHI MESHI OR SHARI)

The first and most important step in making sushi is to prepare the rice! Short grain rice is preferred by the Japanese, as it cooks to a tender and moist grain which clings together. It is indispensable in the making of sushi-meshi. Other types of rice are not suitable—long grain rice is too dry and therefore retains too much water and scented grains are overwhelming in flavour.

One desired outcome in cooking rice for sushi, is that it results in a grain slightly chewier in texture than plain boiled rice. It is typically cooked with a little less water than the usual boiled rice, approximately 10 percent. In order to determine the correct amount of water to be used for cooking the rice, part of the sushi chef's training is to familiarise himself with whether the rice is new rice or old rice, or in fact, whether the rice was grown on the north facing or south facing side of the mountain. All factors which contribute to the internal moisture content of the grain.

However, don't be scared of cooking the rice! Really it is very straightforward. The basic concept is to cook the rice by absorption method and when it is cooked and hot, turn it out into a container and mix through the prepared vinegar solution.

Using a fan to aid in quick cooling is an important step as it helps to ensure the perfect result and produce the glossy sheen that is well regarded.

Whether you use a premium brand Japanese or Californian sushi rice or the common short grain rice readily available from your supermarket, the following recipe will yield an excellent product. If possible, use an electric rice cooker, as the cooking process is then very simple. However, if you do not have one, then choose a heavy bottomed stainless steel saucepan with a tight fitting lid.

PREPARING SUSHI RICE

4 cups	short grain white rice
1.1 lt	water
3 cm sq	kombu

1 Start by washing the rice.

2 Cover with cold water and gently massage with your hand, in order to release the powdered bran and cleaning compound into the water. This will be evidenced by the water becoming a milky colour. If you don't do this, it will result in rice which is covered with a gluey starch and be smelly—both undesirable.

3 Tip most of this off, leaving about one cup.

4 Now, gently agitate and stir the rice for about 10 seconds.

5 Cover with fresh water, swirl to release the starch into the water. Tip off most of the water leaving about one cup and gently agitate as before.

6 Repeat once more.

7 The water should look almost clear. Drain well.

8 Place the rice in the rice cooker with 1.1 litres of water, the kombu and switch on.

9 If you are using a pot to cook the rice in, put the rice and measured water in, cover with the lid and bring to a boil over medium to high heat.

10 Reduce to a medium heat after one minute. When the surface of the rice becomes visible, reduce to a low heat. When all the liquid is absorbed by the rice, turn the heat to high for ten seconds and then turn off the heat.

11 Leave the rice in the pot, covered for a further 15 minutes, to allow the rice to continue to steam. Remove the kombu.

12 Make sure to leave the lid on during the whole cooking process.

VINEGAR DRESSING

100 ml	Japanese rice wine vinegar
60 gm	sugar
20 gm	salt

Prepare the vinegared dressing by dissolving the sugar and salt granules in the vinegar over low heat. Immediately remove from the heat and allow to cool.

Note: A larger amount can be pre-made and stored covered in the refrigerator.

COMBINING THE RICE WITH THE VINEGAR DRESSING

1 Empty the hot rice into a hangiri tub or wide shallow container. Do not allow to cool.

2 Add the prepared vinegar dressing by pouring it over a shamoji or spatula to help disperse the vinegar evenly over the rice.

3 Briefly run the spatula through the rice from top to bottom and left to right in slicing motions, in order to separate the grains and spread the rice.

4 Gather the rice to one side and using horizontal, cutting motions, toss the rice across to the other side in order to give each grain an opportunity to be coated by the vinegar solution.

5 Gather again and repeat making sure not to mash or just stir!

6 Continue to gently toss the rice until it starts to feel just tight. Stop tossing and spread out the rice in an even thin layer.

7 Using a fan, cool the rice to body temperature.

8 Make sure that you turn the rice over so that the bottom heat can be fanned to ensure the vinegar solution is well absorbed.

9 To keep the rice from drying out, place it in a smaller container and cover with a damp cloth.

Congratulations! The rice is now ready for making sushi.

How much rice to cook?

The minimum amount to cook should not be less than two cups of rice.

Even for a professional chef to try and cook one cup of rice is nearly impossible. It's always better to cook too much than not enough!

Cooking four cups of rice as suggested in the recipe will yield approximately 12 cups of prepared sushi-meshi! Whilst this may seem like a lot it is a perfect amount for a sushi dinner party for six people, each person getting some thick roll, thin roll, nigiri-zushi and te-maki-zushi. It will yield about eight futo-maki or thick rolls, or about 20 hoso-maki or thin rolls.

If there is some rice left over, do not refrigerate it, but leave it out wrapped on the bench. Don't worry about it going bad, the vinegar solution in the rice acts as an anti-bacterial agent and it will be fine to use the next day. Prior to use, you can sprinkle over with a little water and then microwave on high until it is just warm to touch.

If you are going to cook more or less than the suggested four cups of rice, remember to alter the vinegar solution accordingly, based on the original recipe.

NOTE:
Your finished sushi-meshi is now very sticky! In order to prevent the rice from sticking all over you while you try to work, it is very important to keep your hands moist with a little 'hand vinegar'.
This is known as tezu and is made by combining ten parts water and 1 part rice vinegar. The sushi chef always has a small bowl close at hand.
Vinegared rice should be eaten the same day it is made—do not refrigerate as it will go hard.

NIGIRI-ZUSHI (SQUEEZED SUSHI)

These are small, hand shaped fingers of rice approximately 20 grams in weight, typically with a topping of seafood of approximately 15 grams.

Nigiri-zushi is representative of Tokyo style food and recognised as the sovereign of the sushi world. Often the word sushi on its own refers to this type. This too is the style that most people imitate when referring to making sushi—typically the index and middle fingers of the right hand are held in the palm of the left hand. Most theories as to the origins of nigiri-zushi suggest they were created by Yohei Hanaya in 1824 in Tokyo, or Edo as it was known at the time. It became known as Edo-mae-zushi, referring to fish caught in front of Edo castle which is today the Imperial palace. There was at that time an abundance of high quality seafood.

Critical in forming good nigiri-zushi, is the correct balance between the topping and the rice and hand-forming by gently squeezing the ingredients together with just the right amount of pressure for the grains to cling and hold together, but loose enough so that it collapses by itself when eaten.

The topping used for nigiri-zushi is known as tane and becomes known as –dane when used with words preceding it. Needless to say, the sushi-dane must be very fresh as they are usually eaten raw. Always obtain the freshest possible fish, asking your fishmonger for sashimi quality.

When you order a sushi main course from the sushi bar, there is a variety of nigiri-zushi presented which actually reflect a commonly used formula of five main groupings or types of tane. These are aka-mi (red meat), shiro-mi (white-meat), hikari-mono (shining tane), nimono (cooked tane) and a group including squid, prawn and various shellfish.

Aka-mi is represented by maguro or tuna and bonito fish. **Shiro-mi** is represented by white fleshed fish such as bream, yellowtail, flounder and whiting.

Hikari-mono are small fish with a shiny skin and is represented by fish such as garfish, sardine and mackerel. Whilst red and white fish are usually eaten raw, shining tane fish are often treated with salt and vinegar prior to use.

Nimono-dane are served after being cooked and spread with tare or nitsume, a viscous seasoned soy sauce. Eel and octopus are perfect examples.

Further to these is a group featuring the roe of salmon, flying fish and sea urchin as well as others. These are presented as gunkan-zushi, a finger of rice circled with a strip of nori seaweed to keep the topping on.

Maguro (tuna)

We will speak in a little depth about this fish as it has become central to nigiri-zushi and indeed is considered king of all tane.

Tuna fish is a classic sushi-dane and the most representative of the red meat tane.

Within the tuna family there are different varieties available, Bluefin being the most highly regarded. Also available are Bigeye and Yellowtail.

Apart from the particular variety of tuna that the maguro for sushi-dane come from, it also depends on which part of the fish is being used.

The tuna parts differ not only in taste, but also in colour and price. You can choose between three different tuna parts.

O-toro is cut from the belly, light coloured and rich in fat. It means 'big fat' and is similar to marbling in beef, with a high infrastructure of internal fat, up to 50 percent. It is soft in flavour and melting in the mouth.
Relative to the rest of the fish, the meat from the belly is scarce and so it is very expensive.

Chu-toro means 'medium fat' and is cut from around the belly. It has less fat and a medium red colour.

Akami is a lean meat, cut from the back of the fish and is deep red in colour. As the back is the most abundant part of the fish, this makes it less expensive than the other cuts.

How to form nigiri-zushi

Before starting, set up your work area with a cutting board, a sharp knife, a small bowl of wasabi and some tezu, vinegared hand water, to moisten the fingers.

Cutting fish into slices of uniform size and thickness appropriate for nigiri-zushi topping takes skill, and can be acquired with practice. Cut fillets crosswise at a slight angle into slices approximately 3-4 cm thick using the sogi-giri cut for sashimi.

Assemble with rice into nigiri as soon as possible.

Dip fingers into tezu and rub hands together to moisten. Shake off any excess.

1 Between the left thumb and forefinger of your left hand, pick up the topping. Lay it along the first joint of the fingers of the left hand, not in the palm.

2 With your right hand, take about 1 1/2 tablespoons of sushi-meshi and gently squeeze into a slightly oval shape

3 Whilst holding the rice in your right palm, use the tip of your right index finger to place a trace of wasabi in the centre of the topping.

4 Place the rice on top of this.

5 Lightly press the top of the rice with your left thumb, leaving a small depression and at the same time, press the ends of the rice with your right thumb and middle finger.

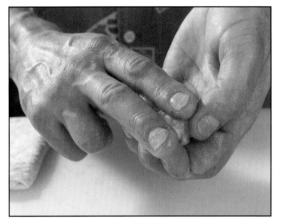

6 Change to press the upper end of the rice with your left thumb while simultaneously pressing across the top of the rice with your right index and middle fingers to firm. The fingers of your left hand should now turn upwards to hold the side of the sushi.

7 Gently roll the finger of sushi across to the right with your right index finger to turn the piece over. The tane will now be facing up.

8 Whilst sliding the piece back to the base of the fingers, give a little squeeze with your right thumb and middle finger on either side of the sushi.

9 Then, gently press the upper end with your left thumb and the topping with your right index and middle fingers. Again, the fingers of your left hand should now turn upwards to hold the side of the sushi.

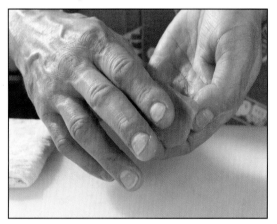

10 Taking the sushi between your right thumb, middle and index fingers, turn the piece 180-degrees to the right.

11 Again, gently press the topping with your right index and middle fingers, as in step 9.

Well done, you now have your nigiri-zushi!

By following these steps and through continued practice you will be able to achieve a good result. Aim at keeping the rice a uniform shape and size and don't pack the rice too tightly.

As an alternative, in the home situation, you can simply mould the rice gently into even shaped fingers, dab each with a little wasabi and then just place the pre-sliced tane on top. Firm gently on top and you will have your nigiri-zushi!

HOW TO EAT NIGIRI-ZUSHI

In years long gone by, sushi was available from indoor shops or outdoor stands, known as yatai. The natural way of eating at that time was by using the fingers. Some say that sushi is the first known finger food. Sushi bars today will always provide chopsticks but many enthusiasts will simply use their fingers as it is easier and time-honored. Choose whichever is more comfortable for you.

Typically when eating nigiri-zushi, either turn it over so the fish is on the bottom, or on its side, and then dip the fish side lightly into the soy sauce. Eat it in one or two bites.

Under no circumstances should you dip the rice side into the soy sauce. The taste of soy will be overpowering and the rice will fall apart!

Sushi is always accompanied by gari, pickled ginger, to refresh the palate in between different types of seafood. Traditionally sushi is also accompanied by hot green tea. This also helps to prepare the mouth for the next serving by removing any aftertaste and oil.

In modern sushi shops, alcoholic drinks are readily available. Sake and beer are commonly enjoyed with sushi but white wines such as sauvignon blanc or chardonnay also complement the flavours of sushi.

If you are ordering from the sushi bar, there is no set order in eating nigiri-zushi, really it is up to you to choose. Start communicating with the sushi chef by asking what tane is recommended or why not try being adventurous and ask the chef to serve you according to their whim, omakase, and you will receive the finest selection of the day. Asking for 'jo-nigiri' will also ensure the best quality, as jo- means first or best!

Itadakimasu … the Japanese equivalent to bon apetit, simply an acknowledgement for what they are about to receive.

GUNKAN-ZUSHI

As mentioned earlier, some toppings for nigiri-zushi will not stay in place on top of the rice—typically salmon roe, flying fish roe and sea urchin roe. Gunkan-zushi was created to hold them in place and consists of vertically wrapping a strip of nori around the finger of rice, ensuring that it is wide enough to project 1–2 cm above the level of the rice.

1 You will need strips of nori 15 cm x 3 cm, one strip for each gunkan-zushi.

2 Prepare fingers of sushi rice as per nigiri-zushi, rice only! Try to make each one uniform in size and shape.

3 Top each finger of rice with a smear of wasabi.

4 Start by pressing one end of the nori to the rice and wrap vertically

around the rice, shiny side facing out. Keep your hands as dry as possible when handling the nori.

5 Seal the overlapping end of the nori with a grain of rice as glue

6 Place the filling inside the top.

One suggested way to eat gunkan is to brush the top with a bit of gari that has been dipped in shoyu as you can't turn this one upside down.

Gunkan translates as battleship or warship, the name probably given because it is thought to resemble that in shape.

MAKI-ZUSHI (ROLLED SUSHI)

Literally 'rolled sushi', maki-zushi is the general name for all sushi that is rolled.

They are made by wrapping sushi rice and ingredients in toasted nori sheets and shaping with a makisu, a bamboo rolling mat. They are often referred to as nori-maki, meaning rolled in nori.

This rolled style of sushi is easy to make and can be assembled with your own preferred fillings. Whilst there are classical ingredients or combinations used at the sushi bar, small kitchen adventures can be equally delicious. They are easy to eat and very popular as an appetiser or snack or as a lunchtime food, evidenced by their profusion now at food courts and snack bars.

According to their size and shape, sushi rolls are classed as hoso-maki, thin rolls or futo-maki, thick rolls.

Thin nori-maki is 2.5 cm in diameter and usually contains one main ingredient. Only half a sheet of nori is used to make hoso-maki and you will get six bite size rounds from each roll.

While nori-maki are usually rolled in a bamboo mat, the exception is te-maki-zushi, a thin rolled sushi that is rolled by hand into a cone shape and eaten as made.

Thick nori-maki is 5 cm in diameter and contains about five core ingredients. When ordered at the sushi bar, futo-maki is made with a half sheet of nori and rolled lengthwise. It yields four slices from each roll.

There is a type of maki-zushi which does not use nori seaweed. These are known as bou-zushi. A bou is a long cylindrical piece of wood or pole used in martial art stick fighting.

Sushi rice is fashioned into a long baton shape, topped with ingredients and firmed and rolled with plastic wrap and a makisu. A recipe for one example of this style is included, known as tazuna-zushi.

NOTE:

It is important to note that nori has a 'presentation' side which is smooth and shiny and a 'back' side, which has a rougher texture. When rolling maki-zushi, the shiny side is always put down onto the mat so when it is rolled, it will be on the outside.

Sushi rolls should be eaten soon after they are made as the nori quickly absorbs moisture from the rice and loses its crispness.

HOW TO CUT NORI-MAKI

The key to cutting nori-maki is to first dip the end of your knife into the bowl of tezu hand vinegar and point the knife up so as to allow a bead of water to run down the edge of the knife. This prevents the knife from sticking. Be sure to wipe the blade clean in between cuttings.

Make sure to put the sushi roll on the cutting board with the 'seam' facing down. Hoso-maki are first cut into half and then each half into three pieces. These are then served with the core upward. For futo-maki made with a half sheet, they are first cut into half and then each half is cut into two pieces.

Serve with shoyu as a dipping sauce.

Hoso-maki (thin sushi rolls)

These three are the most typical of thin sushi rolls.

Tekka-maki (tuna rolls)

Mukashi, mukashi … in the olden days, gambling dens were known as tekka-ba. To prevent the fingers of the gamblers from getting sticky, the sushi chefs created these nori rolls featuring tuna and with the passing of time they became known as tekka-maki.

Makes 4 rolls (24 pieces)

2	nori sheets
100 gm	tuna, raw
300 gm	sushi rice
2 tspn	wasabi paste

1 Cut each nori sheet in half lengthwise. Each half sheet will yield one roll.

2 Cut tuna into strips, each measuring approximately 1.5 x 1.5 x 18 cm.

3 Place a sheet of nori, shiny side down, on bamboo rolling mat..

4 Moisten your fingers and palms with tezu and shake off any excess.

5 Take about 75 gm prepared sushi rice and spread it over the nori sheet from edge to edge, but make sure to leave a blank strip at the top of 1 cm and at the bottom of the sheet of 1/2 cm, uncovered. The layer should be 3/4–1 cm in thickness.

6 Take care to spread it evenly and don't firm too hard to compact the rice.

7 Moisten your hands again as required, to prevent rice sticking to your fingers.

8 With your fingers, make a groove across the centre of the rice and using your index finger, smear a thin line of wasabi in the groove from one side across to the other.

9 Lay 1/4 of the strips of tuna across the wasabi and then position the nori sheet close to you in line with the edge of the bamboo mat.

10 Hold the tuna in place with your fingertips. Using your thumbs lift the front of the mat closest to you up and over and continue this forward rolling motion so rice meets rice.

11 Lift up the top of the mat and roll over a little more, so the strip of nori at the far end is now on the bottom of the roll.

12 Squeeze gently to firm the roll and shape each end with your fingers so that no rice will fall out.

13 Place the roll on a chopping board and use the remaining ingredients to assemble three more rolls.

14 Cut each roll in half and then each half into three equal pieces. Allow six pieces per serve.

Kappa-maki (cucumber rolls)

In Japanese legends, kappas were mischievous water fairies whose favourite food is cucumber. Cucumber rolls were named kappa-maki in honour of the kappa.

Makes 4 rolls (24 pieces)

2	nori sheets
100 gm	cucumber julienne
340 gm	sushi rice
2 tspn	wasabi paste
2 tspn	sesame seeds, toasted to a light golden colour

1 Choose the smaller variety of cucumber, as they tend to have a clearer flavour and softer skin than the longer types. They are sometimes known as Lebanese cucumber in various countries. It should be crisp and the skin firm.

2 Prepare the cucumber by first washing and drying.

3 Cut into thin strips about 8 cm long, and then into julienne, match-like strips.

4 Using the skin is perfectly fine, but avoid the seeds.

5 Proceed with the cucumber rolls in the same way as the tuna rolls.

6 Replace the tuna with the cucumber and give a light sprinkling of sesame seeds before rolling.

Variations:
Try also with a shiso leaf and a smear of umeboshi plum paste or a little Japanese mayonnaise.

Note:
The world record for the longest sushi is held by the Nikopaka Festa Committee. In October 1997, they achieved the feat of making a kappa-maki at Yoshii, Japan, that was 1136 metres long!

Kampyo-maki
(seasoned gourd strip roll)

This traditional sushi uses seasoned strips of pith

from the gourd or calabash and is much loved by

the Japanese. It is sometimes known as teppo-maki,

gun roll, as it resembles a gun barrel.

For preparing kampyo:

30 gm	kampyo, raw
375 ml	dashi
60 ml	shoyu
60 gm	sugar
40 ml	mirin

1 Wash and lightly knead the kampyo with a little salt to soften the fibres.

2 Rinse well and simmer in water for ten minutes. Drain very well, squeezing out all the water.

3 Combine dashi, shoyu and sugar and bring to simmer. Add the kampyo and continue to gently simmer until the colour has changed and the flavour absorbed.

4 Be careful not to overcook it as it will all break apart. When soft to the fingernail, remove from the liquid to cool.

5 Now bring the liquid to a boil and reduce to a light syrup. Remove from the heat and add the mirin. Cool completely.

6 Cut the kampyo into 18 cm lengths and store in the liquid until ready to use.

Makes 4 rolls (24 pieces)

2	nori sheets
100 gm	kampyo
340 gm	sushi rice

1 Proceed with the kampyo-maki in the same way as the tuna rolls, replacing the tuna with the kampyo.

2 Make sure to gently squeeze kampyo of any excess liquid prior to rolling.

Note:
This maki-zushi does not use wasabi.

Vegetarian options

With such a variety, Asian commodities and dishes lend themselves very well to present as vegetarian options.

Choose from the following as a start but experiment with what is on hand and let your imagination help you to discover delicious combinations that you'll come back to time and time again.

Try grilled fresh mushrooms and spring onion, sweetened omelette strips, blanched spinach, seasoned shiitake, blanched asparagus, avocado slices, carrot julienne, sliced pickled radish, various salad leaves, sliced tofu, sprouts, snow peas, etc.

Te-maki-zushi (hand rolled sushi)

Literally translates as hand rolled sushi. This rolled sushi variation is presented in a cone form and can be enjoyed easily at home.

Simply take a piece of nori seaweed, top with sushi-meshi and filling ingredients and roll into a cone shape.

They are quick and easy to prepare and taste delicious, as they are eaten as soon as they are made, so the nori is still crisp.

Te-maki-zushi are eaten as is, without being cut. Half a sheet is typically used and produces sushi the size of an ice cream cone. A quarter sheet makes a smaller roll but has the advantage of allowing you to experiment with many different fillings.

Small te-maki are ideal as appetisers as they are easily eaten with fingers.

Invite your friends for a sushi party as a fun way to enjoy sushi. Each of your guests can combine ingredients according to their own preference.

Note:
Te-maki-zushi can also be rolled up into a cylinder shape.

Makes 10 rolls

600 gm	sushi-meshi
5 sheets	nori seaweed
50 gm	shiitake mushroom, prepared as for futo-maki-zushi
50 gm	cucumber julienne
150 gm	salmon, raw, cut into strips
10 sprigs	watercress or shiso leaves
5 tspn	mayo
2 tspn	gari, chopped
2 tspn	wasabi

1 Prepare nori sheets by cutting across in half. Divide each of the ingredients into ten portions.

2 Moisten your right hand but keep your left hand dry (reverse if you are left handed).

3 Start by picking up a sheet in your left hand. Place a 60 gm oblong shaped ball of rice on the left hand side of the nori.

4 Flatten the rice and make a groove down the middle. Smear with a little wasabi.

5 Working quickly, place a leaf on the rice, followed by the salmon. Add a little mayonnaise and follow with some mushroom, cucumber and a sprinkle of chopped ginger.

6 Fold the nearest corner (bottom, left hand side) over the filling and with the help of your right hand, bring it up to meet the top edge of nori.

7 Firm in around the ingredients and then continue to roll around to result in a cone.

8 Use remaining ingredients to make more cones.

Shake over with a little soy sauce and eat immediately.

SOME COMMON INGREDIENTS

prawn meat, cooked

cucumber, cut into julienne

asparagus spears, blanched

carrot, cut into julienne

kampyo strips

chicken teriyaki cut into pieces

avocado

omelette

herbs, sprouts and salad leaves

pickles

smoked salmon and lemon juice

eel, cooked

duck, roasted

grilled salmon skin

roast beef

crab

sea urchin roe, salmon roe or flying fish roe

tuna, raw or cooked

salmon, raw or cooked

snow peas or green beans, blanched and cut julienne

mayonnaise or umeboshi plum paste

toasted sesame seeds

Really, the possibilities are endless. Through trial and error you will discover new and exciting combinations.

Futo-maki-zushi (thick sushi rolls)

Maki-sushi are a refined and exciting delicacy and a visual delight, none more so than futo-maki. In fact at one time they were known as date-maki, dandy rolls.

There are two types of futo-maki, the common variety with the seaweed on the outside, and ura-maki, otherwise known as 'inside-out' rolls. This is where the order of ingredients is reversed, so the nori is on the inside and the rice is on the outside! The most famous example of this is the California roll.

At the sushi bar, futo-maki are typically made with half a sheet of nori seaweed. For the recipes that follow, a full sheet of nori seaweed is used.

NOTE:
These maki-zushi typically do not have wasabi.

Futomaki

Makes 2 rolls (16 pieces)

2 sheets	nori seaweed
8	large, dried shiitake mushrooms
60 gm	kampyo, prepared gourd ribbons
100 gm	spinach leaves
60 gm	sweetened omelette
4 cups	prepared sushi rice
100 gm	salmon fillet, raw
1 tblspn	Japanese mayonnaise

For simmering mushrooms:

500 ml	water
100 ml	soy sauce
100 gm	sugar
50 ml	Sake
1/2 tspn	instant dashi granules
20 ml	mirin

1 Gently simmer mushrooms in water for one hour until tender. Keep topping up the level of liquid as required.

2 Add dashi, soy, sake and sugar and bring to boiling point.

3 Continue to simmer mushrooms in liquid, until the liquid is a light syrup.

4 Remove from heat and add the mirin.

5 Set aside to cool. Remove the mushrooms from the liquid, cut off the stalks and discard, and slice the mushrooms. Store in the liquid until ready to use.

6 Squeeze off any excess liquid prior to use.

For simmering kampyo:

Prepare kampyo as for previous recipe for kampyo-maki.

To prepare salmon fillet:

Cut salmon fillet into strips 1.5 cm x 1.5 cm x 20 cm.

For simmering spinach:

200 gm spinach leaves

Wash the leaves well. Bring a large pot of lightly salted water to the boil, add the spinach and cook briefly until it is limp and the colour brightens. Remove and plunge into iced water. Drain well and gently wring out all the water.

To prepare omelette:

2	eggs
40 ml	dashi
pinch	salt
2 tspn	mirin
1 tspn	usukuchi, light soy sauce

1 Beat the eggs to combine the whites and yolks. Add the other ingredients and mix well. Strain.

2 Using a non stick fry pan, proceed to cook as a thin omelette or as crepes, until the mix is exhausted. Slice finely.

TO ASSEMBLE:

1 First moisten your hands with the hand-vinegar and shake off any excess.

2 Place one sheet of toasted nori (shiny side down) on bamboo sushi mat. Spread two cups of prepared sushi rice evenly over the nori sheet, leaving 2 cm free across the far end.

3 Spread half the mayonnaise across the rice.

4 Lay the ingredients across the centre in rows starting at a point about 1/3 up.

5 Holding the line of ingredients gently in place with your fingers, push up and turn over the end of the bamboo mat closest to you with your thumbs, so the edge of the nori meets the rice on the other side of the filling. Gently firm.

6 Lift up the top of the mat and continue to roll, so the strip of nori on the top side is now on the bottom of the roll.

7 Squeeze gently to firm and shape the roll. Firm in the ends with your fingers so that no rice will fall out.

8 Use remaining ingredients to assemble one more roll.

TO SERVE:

As a rule the roll is cut in half and each half into four pieces. Remember to wet the knife and do not saw through the roll.

URA-MAKI-ZUSHI (INSIDE OUT ROLLS)

CALIFORNIA ROLL

As the name implies, this roll was created by a chef in California on America's west coast. They call for fillings of crab meat, ripe avocado, cucumber strips and Japanese mayonnaise and are totally delicious.

Makes 2 rolls (16 pieces)

2 sheets	nori seaweed
5 cups	prepared sushi rice
1/2	avocado
1/2	cucumber
120 gm	crab meat, cooked
1 tblspn	Japanese mayonnaise
2 tblspn	flying fish roe or tobikko
	plastic wrap

1 Prior to rolling, spend a moment searching through the crab meat with your fingers and remove any shell that might be remaining.

2 Slice the avocado into strips.

3 Cut the cucumber into julienne strips, as for kappa-maki.

4 Cover the bamboo rolling mat with a sheet of plastic wrap.

5 Place a sheet of nori on the mat and spread half the rice over the entire sheet, from edge to edge.

6 Now turn the rice-covered nori sheet upside down onto the sushi mat.

7 The rice will now be facing down and the nori sheet up.

8 Spread some mayonnaise across the middle of the nori sheet.

9 Then place half the avocado, cucumber, and crab meat on top.

10 Start rolling the mat up over the ingredients and roll almost one complete turn, stopping to press and firm and then complete the roll as for futo-maki.

11 Make sure the plastic wrap doesn't get rolled in!

12 Remove the plastic wrap and using a spoon, place a coating of roe evenly over the rice.

13 Gently cut as for futo-maki.

14 Use remaining ingredients to assemble one more roll.

You may substitute the crab meat with some cooked king prawn meat.

You may substitute toasted white sesame seeds for the flying fish roe.

This is also very nice with a little chopped gari, pickled ginger, sprinkled in with the filling.

Tazuna-zushi

Tazuna-zushi translates as reins or bridle and refers to coils of a rope, or striations. It is characterised by its tri-coloured rope pattern.

Although still a rolled sushi, this maki-zushi does not use nori and is simpler and easier to make!

Basically, you form a long cylinder shape of prepared sushi rice and top with a variety of colouful ingredients. Adjust the shape with plastic wrap and a makisu.

Makes 2 rolls

400 gm	**sushi rice**
6	**King prawns, green**
1 small	**cucumber**
1 tspn	**gari, pickled ginger, very fine slices**
8	**baby whiting fillets**

TO PREPARE THE PRAWNS:

1. Remove the head and insert a bamboo skewer just under the shell along the leg side, into the tail.

2. Bring a small pot of salted water to the boil and add the prawns. When it returns to a boil, simmer for two minutes and remove to iced water.

3. When completely chilled, draw out the skewer with a twisting motion. Do not remove the skewer when warm, as the prawn will curl again.

4. Pull off the pointed, sharp piece above the tail and remove all the shell leaving the tail on.

5. Neatly trim the head side and then make a deep butterfly cut from the belly side nearly all the way through and open the prawn.

6. Gently flatten and wash away the vein in lightly salted and vinegared water. Drain well.

7. Cut into two pieces lengthwise.

To prepare the cucumber:

Wash well and then dry. Leave the skin on and cut lengthwise into thin strips. A Japanese mandolin is perfect for this. Sprinkle with a little salt and leave for 15 minutes to soften. Rinse well and drain.

To prepare the whiting:

Ensure all bones are removed. Lay the fillets out on a board, skin side down and cover with kitchen toweling paper. Sprinkle over with an even rain of salt. Leave for 30 minutes. This is a Japanese technique known as kami-jio, used to achieve a more delicate seasoning. Rinse the fillets and then let stand in rice vinegar for five minutes. Peel off the skin from the head end.

To assemble:

Cover the bamboo rolling mat with plastic wrap. Alternately position the ingredients diagonally across the plastic, presentation side down, being mindful of colour arrangement.

Place the prawn first, then the cucumber, then the whiting, repeating in this way across the mat.

Smear across with some wasabi and sprinkle with slivers of ginger.

Form a cylinder with half the rice, about the width of the makisu, as evenly as you can and place across the middle.

Roll almost one complete turn and then pause to press and firm.

Finish the roll so that the ingredients are on top.

Firm in the ends and allow to set for a minute. Cut with the plastic wrap on, and then remove the plastic to serve. Assemble one more roll with remaining ingredients.

This style of sushi typically features seafood, but is equally successful with various vegetables arranged in a similar manner.

CHIRASHI-ZUSHI (SCATTERED SUSHI)

Chirashi-zushi translates as scattered sushi. Typically it is a bowl of sushi rice with a variety of flavoured, cooked or raw ingredients scattered on top.

Following are two recipes: edo-mae-chirashi, which represents the Tokyo form where the ingredients are artistically placed on top of the sushi-meshi and bara-chirashi-zushi, as it is known in the Kansai district of Osaka and Kyoto, where the ingredients are mixed in with the rice.

Although chirashi-zushi is often made including sashimi, it is also commonly seen without any seafood as o-bento, or lunch boxes, taken on picnics and sold at railway stations and food take-aways. Vegetarian chirashi-zushi is also readily available.

NOTE:
Typically, when you order chirashi-zushi at a sushi bar, it will come in the Tokyo form.

EDO-MAE-CHIRASHI

Serves 2

400 gm	sushi-meshi
2 slices	tuna, cut sogi-giri style as for sashimi
2 slices	salmon, cut sogi-giri style as for sashimi
2 slices	yellowtail kingfish, cut sogi-giri style as for sashimi
2 pieces	prawns, cooked as for tazuna-zushi but leave the tail on for decoration.
2 whole	cooked shiitake mushrooms, prepared as for futo-maki, but left whole
4 strips	kampyo, prepared as for futo-maki, chopped into small pieces
1/2 sheet	nori seaweed, shredded by cutting with a knife or scissors
1 small	cucumber sliced as a garnish
60 gm	omelette, prepared as for futo-maki, but cooked as a thick piece
3 whole	green shiso leaves
1 tblspn	oboro (see ingredients list)
4 pieces	snow peas, blanched
1 tspn	wasabi paste
1 tblspn	gari

1 Place the rice into a lacquered bowl or container and sprinkle over with the oboro, kampyo and nori.

2 Arrange the prawns, omelette, snow peas and shiitake mushrooms at the back.

3 Lean the shiso leaves against these and then arrange the tuna, salmon and kingfish slices.

4 Decorate with a mound of wasabi, and pickled ginger and the cucumber.

BARA-CHIRASHI-ZUSHI

Serves 2

400 gm	prepared sushi rice
40 gm	kampyo, sliced
40 gm	shiitake, sliced
1 tblspn	ao-nori
1 tblspn	white sesame seeds, toasted
50 gm	tuna, diced
50 gm	salmon, diced
50 gm	white fish, diced
1 tblspn	tobikko, flying fish roe
40 gm	cucumber, julienne
20 gm	takuan, finely sliced
1 tblspn	gari, finely sliced
2 sheets	nori
40 gm	sweet omelette, finely sliced
1 tspn	wasabi

1 Prepare all ingredients separately.

2 Gently mix the rice, kampyo, shiitake, sesame seeds, ao-nori, cucumber, takuan and gari together in a large bowl. Take care not to mash the ingredients. Loosely place into serving bowls.

3 Combine the tuna, salmon, white fish and tobikko together and place on top of the rice.

4 Scatter over with the sliced omelette.

5 Toast the nori sheets lightly over a flame and crush between your hands directly on top of the omelette.

6 Serve with a mound of wasabi to one side.

As a variation, the fish can be cooked or marinated.

It's important to make mention of two well loved presentations of chirashi-zushi: tekka-don and sake-don.

1 Tekka as the name implies, is to do with tuna and -don is a shortening of donburi, or deep bowl. Tekka-don then, is a style of chirashi-zushi featuring tuna sashimi slices only, placed on top of the rice.

2 Sake-don has the same style of presentation but features salmon sashimi instead.

OSHI-ZUSHI (PRESSED SUSHI)

Literally translated, oshi-zushi means press molded sushi. Sushi in the Kansai region, encompassing Osaka and Kyoto, has a longer history of sushi than Tokyo, of the Kanto region. Here hako-zushi, boxed sushi, has been enjoyed for a very long time and the residents take great pleasure in pressed mackerel sushi. This style of sushi tends to feature more cooked than raw seafood.

In the absence of the special cypress box required for this pressed sushi, substitute with say, a cake tin, lined with plastic wrap.

EBI-OSHI-ZUSHI

This is simple to make and will impress your friends at a dinner party!

1 kg	sushi rice
16	medium prawns, prepared as for tazuna zushi
2 sheets	nori
1 tblspn	wasabi paste
1 tblspn	gari
10	shiso leaves

1 Prepare a 20 cm round cake tin by lining with plastic wrap.

2 Place the prawns on the plastic wrap, belly side up, in a circular pattern with the tails touching in the centre.

3 Smear each prawn with a little wasabi.

4 Spread half the sushi rice evenly over the prawns and then cover with the nori and press down to firm. Sprinkle over the gari.

5 Evenly spread the remainder of the rice over the nori, cover with extra plastic wrap and firm down. Remove the plastic.

6 Arrange a plate with the shiso leaves evenly around the rice with the tops 2-3 cm beyond the edge. Place a plate directly over the sushi and invert the lot. Gently remove the tin and the plastic wrap.

7 Simply cut into wedges to eat.

Feel free to substitute the prawns with any other seafood, raw or cooked, or vegetables, and assemble in the same manner.

MISO SOUP

No meal is complete without at least one bowl of soup. The popular miso soup is often enjoyed with sushi. Miso is a fermented soy bean paste and there are many varieties. Typically, the darker the colour, the saltier the miso; the white types of miso being less salty and sweet.

The combination of tofu, wakame and spring onion is classic to the Japanese, but feel free to experiment with other ingredients.

Serves 6

1 lt	**water**
1 tspn	**dashi granules**
90 gm	**miso, white, Inaka style**
90 gm	**tofu, diced**
10 gm	**wakame seaweed, reconstituted and squeezed dry**
2 tblspn	**spring onion, finely chopped**

1 Bring the water to the boil and add the dashi granules. Turn the heat to very low, and gently whisk in the miso paste. Do not boil.
2 Place tofu and wakame seaweed into soup bowls and pour over the hot soup. Garnish with spring onion.

HEALTH AND SUSHI

Sushi is commended by nutritionists worldwide as being a balanced and nourishing food! Here is a food low in calories, high in protein and moderate in carbohydrates. Let's have a look at the main ingredients.

Rice is an excellent source of dietary fibre and complex carbohydrates, providing energy for the body.

Fish and seafood deliver a full spectrum of nutrients and are an excellent source of protein. All seafood is low in kilojoules and rich in vitamins. It is also an excellent source of minerals including iodine, zinc and potassium, and rich in Omega-3 fatty acids.

Nori seaweed is high in protein and vitamins, particularly the B group and also minerals, notably calcium, iron, phosphorus and iodine.

Vinegar, ginger and wasabi are all well known for their antibacterial properties. Wasabi helps to stimulate the secretion of saliva and digestive juices and is an excellent source of vitamin C. Soy sauce contains many amino acids and an array of vitamins, mainly B1 and B2.

Without a doubt, sushi can be seen to promote health and easily fits in with modern day eating habits of people.

CONCLUSION

Congratulations on purchasing *Simply Sushi*. You should by now be feeling somewhat more confident about what sushi is and better equipped to make an excellent presentation in your home.

Whilst sushi is recognised as being a healthy food, remember that healthy eating is as much to do with the atmosphere as the ingredients. Good friends around the table enjoying beautiful food makes for a memorable occasion and indeed you can digest food better this way! So invite your friends over for a casual meal and have fun, relax and try not to get too disillusioned if your first efforts aren't as wonderful as you might like them to be—practice makes perfect!

At the sushi bar feel free to ask questions of the sushi chef—not just about the food but also try and get some tips. Part of the training for a sushi chef is in interpersonal skills and developing a relationship with the customer is welcomed.

At the end of your meal, it is appropriate to acknowledge your thanks for a delightful meal with 'gochiso sama deshita'!

I'd like to take this opportunity to thank my family, Colleen, Eleanor and Wilson for their patience and support, and my friend Trudy, Fran, Melinda, John and Lynn, and especially Mr.Yamakoshi for their encouragement and help, without whom this project would not be possible.

Thanks again and here's to many wonderful meals of sushi.

ABOUT THE AUTHOR

Steven started his cooking career in 1976. He did his apprenticeship at Stephanie's restaurant in Melbourne under the guidance of Stephanie Alexander.

Steven left in 1984 to be chef at Tatler's Café in Sydney with his good friend Tony Tan, before returning to Stephanie's to be Head Chef for two years.

In 1987 Steven started at Kenzan Japanese restaurant and studied intensively with Master Kaiseki Chef, Mr Yamakoshi and Itamae-san at the sushi bar, Mr Yoshizumi.

In 1993 Steven started teaching at William Angliss Institute, where he is currently co-ordinator of the Level 3 Apprentice Cooks and the Great Chefs Program.

Together with Mr Yamakoshi and Mr Yoshizumi, Steven presented the very successful Sushi Crawl for 3 years as part of the Melbourne Food and Wine Festival and was a presenter at the Master Class at the Grand Hyatt.

He continues to run various classes on sushi and hopes this book will encourage others to try their hand.